The VIRTUOSIC CHRISTMAS PERFORMER

8 Impressive Carol Arrangements for
Intermediate to Late Intermediate Pianists

MARGARET GOLDSTON

The arrangements in *The Virtuosic Christmas Performer* are showy solos intended to inspire both church congregations and recital audiences alike. The solos abound with impressive scale passages, big-sounding chords, lush harmonies and interesting rhythms. Intermediate to late intermediate pianists will find these arrangements motivating to learn and perform.

The medley in "Away in a Manger" creatively weaves the two different tunes of this carol together. "The Songs of Christmas" features a medley of four carols that includes "Sing We Now of Christmas," "Angels We Have Heard on High," "Joy to the World" and "Hark! the Herald Angels Sing." This arrangement is suitable for those occasions when a longer solo is needed, such as for a church prelude or postlude.

The many requests I had from teachers and students for a more advanced Christmas collection inspired me to write these arrangements. I hope that they, in turn, inspire exciting performances of these favorite Christmas carols.

Enjoy a most blessed Christmas!

Alfred

Copyright © MMI by Alfred Publishing Co., Inc.
All rights reserved. Printed in USA.
ISBN 0-7390-2287-3

Silent Night

Franz Grüber
Arr. by Margaret Goldston

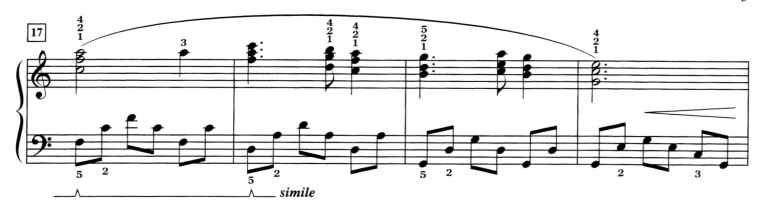

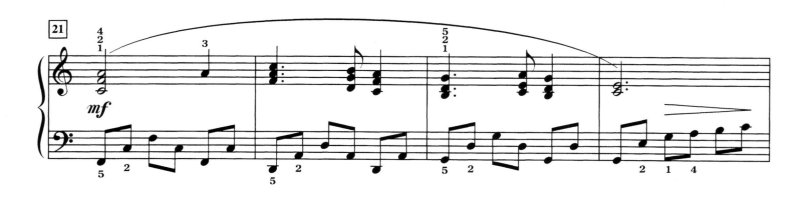

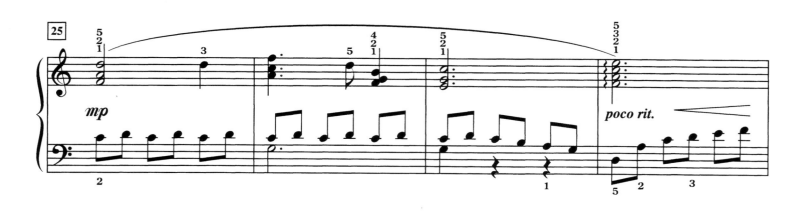

Carol of the Bells

M. Leontovich
Arr. by Margaret Goldston

8

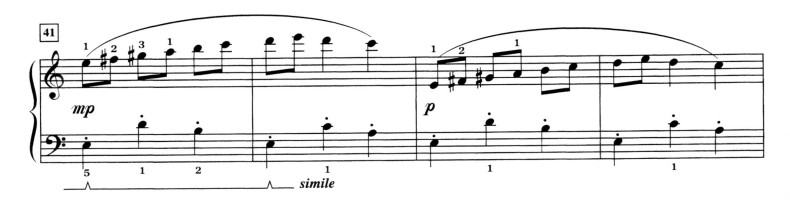

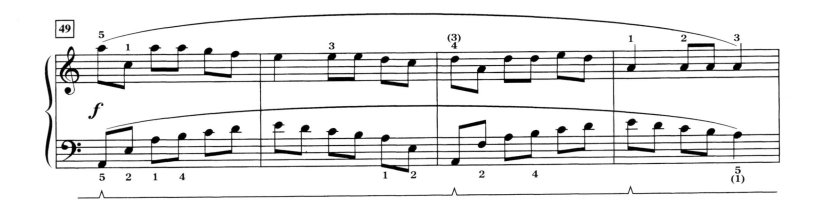

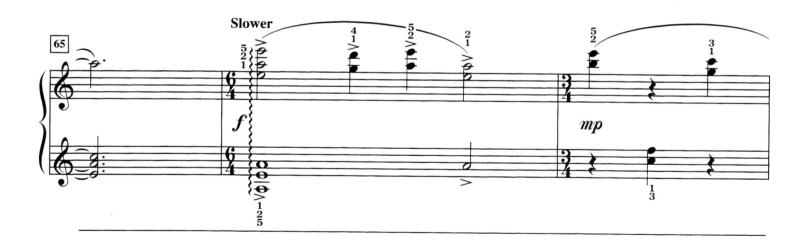

Away in a Manger *

1st tune: J. E. Spillman
2nd tune: James R. Murray
Arr. by Margaret Goldston

* This arrangement interweaves two tunes of *Away in a Manger.* The first tune appears at the beginning of the piece; the second tune enters in the right hand of measure 16 as the left hand continues with the first tune.

Sounds of Christmas

A Medley of Four Carols

Arr. by Margaret Goldston

SING WE NOW OF CHRISTMAS (Traditional French Melody)

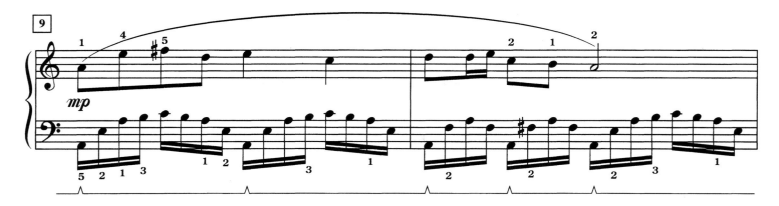

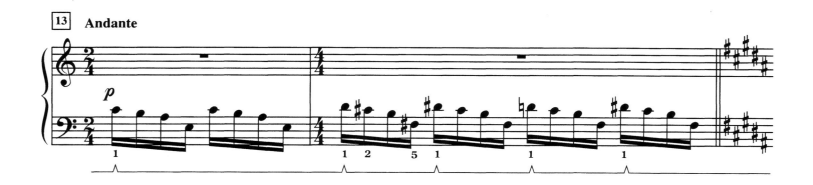

ANGELS WE HAVE HEARD ON HIGH (Traditional French Melody)

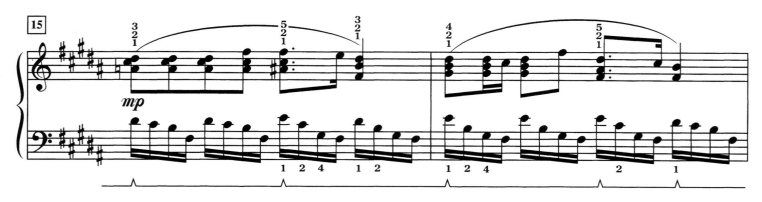

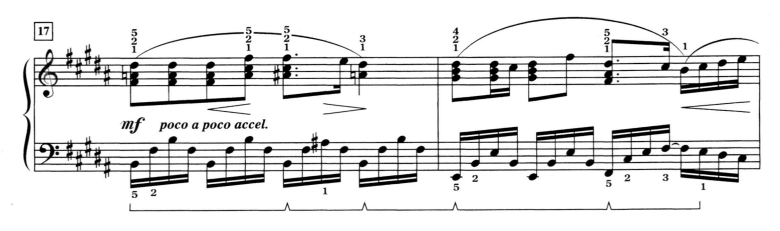

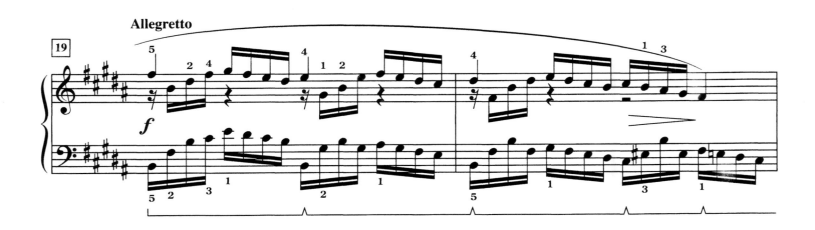

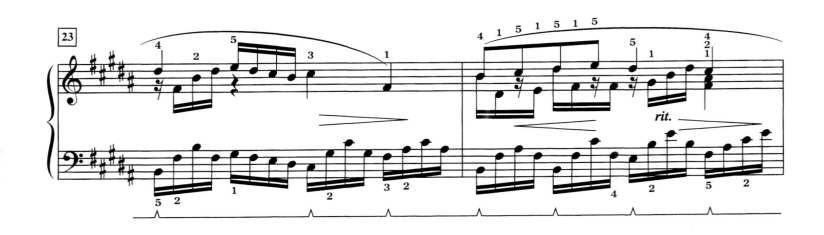

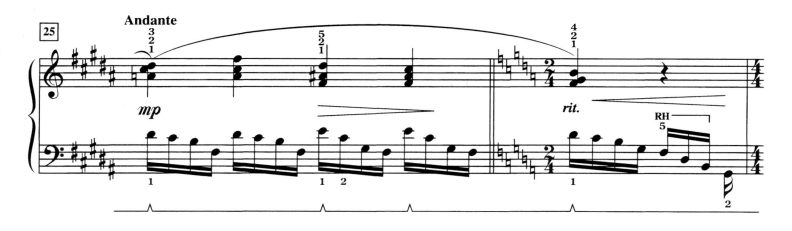

JOY TO THE WORLD (George F. Handel)

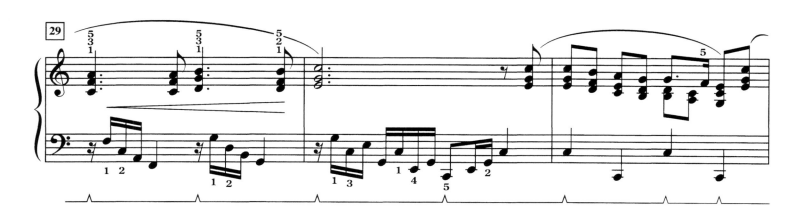

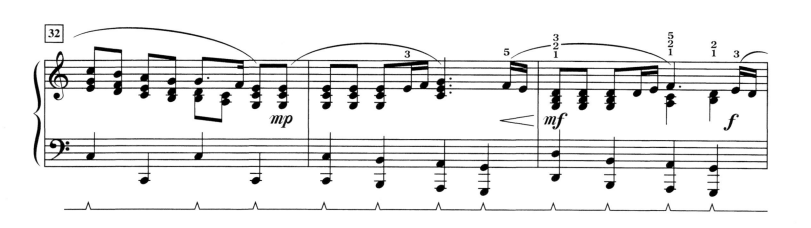

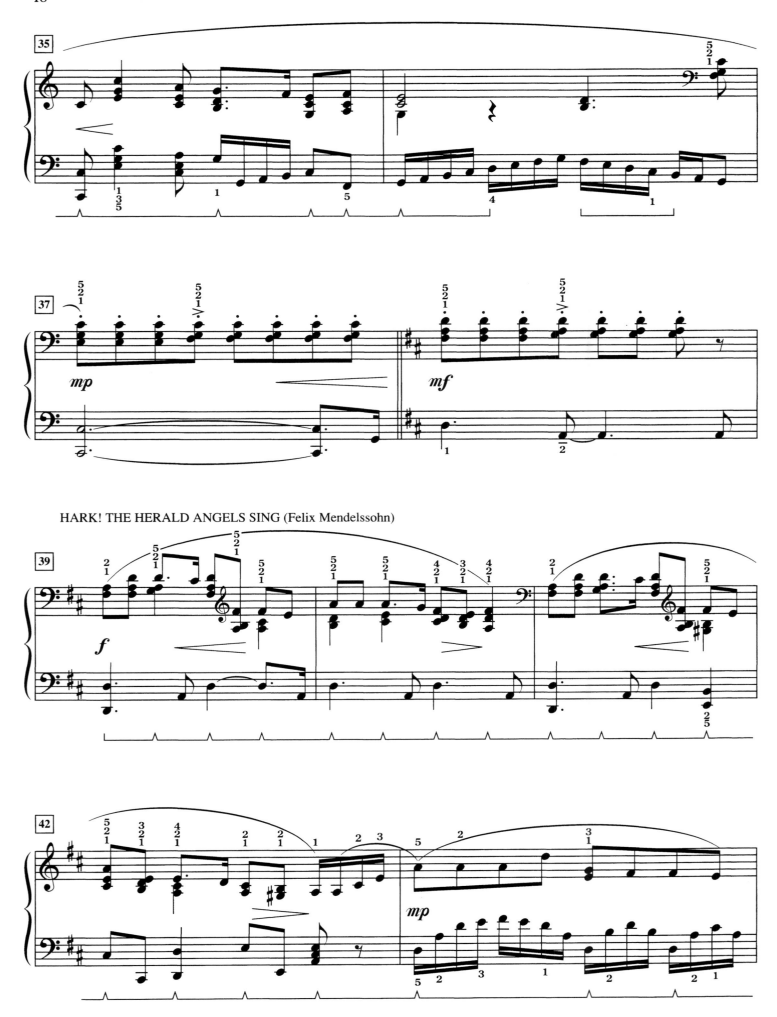

HARK! THE HERALD ANGELS SING (Felix Mendelssohn)

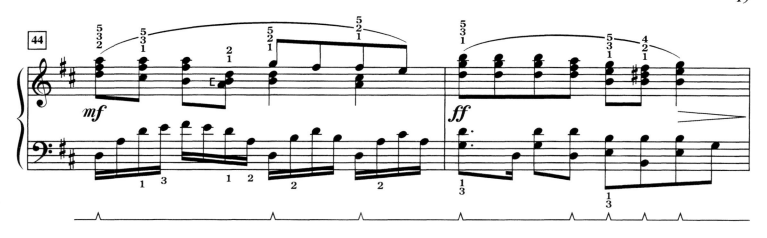

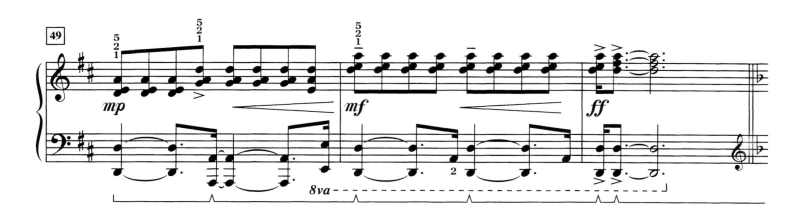

OPTIONAL CODA

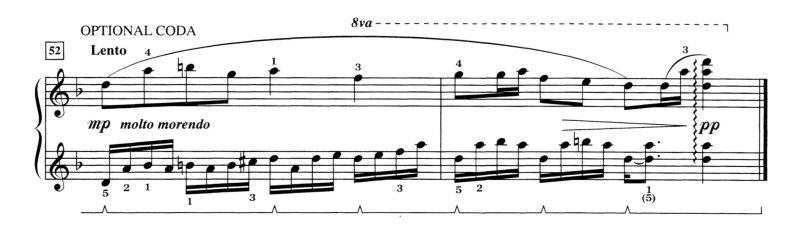

What Child Is This?

Old English Melody
Arr. by Margaret Goldston

Moderately, flowing

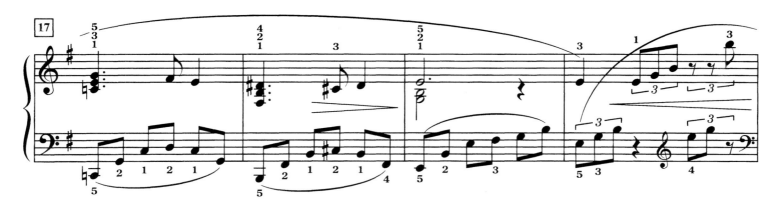

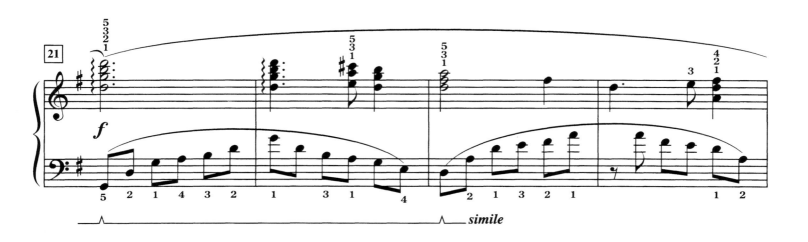

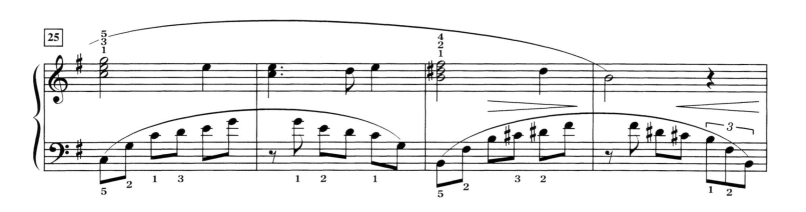

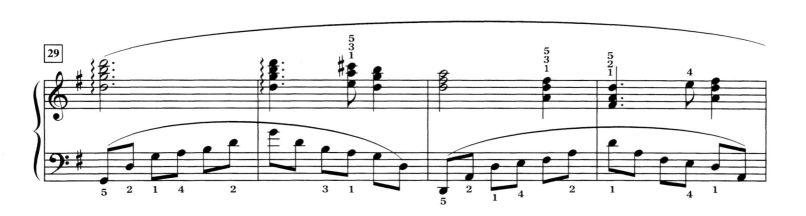

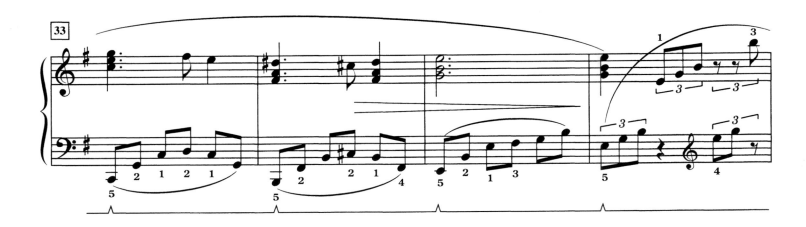

Meno mosso

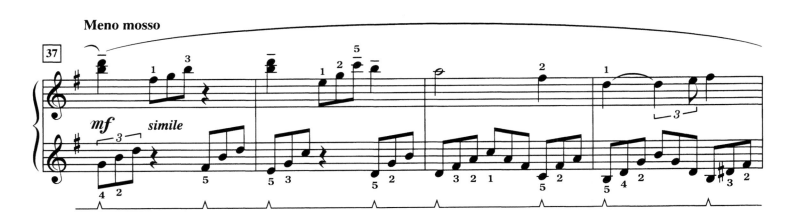

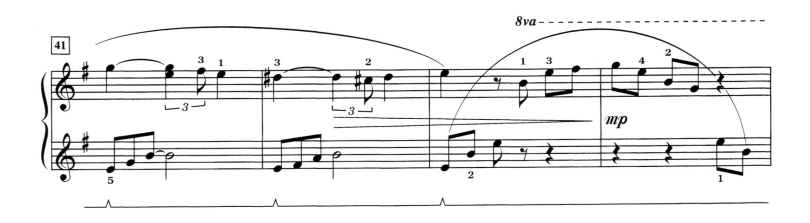

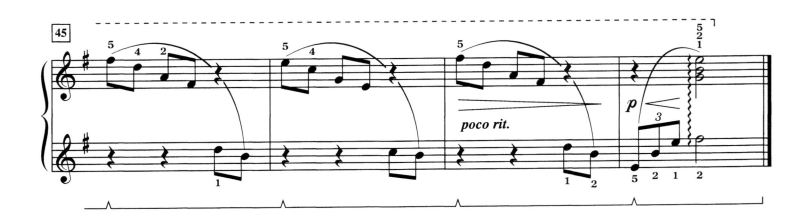

O Come, All Ye Faithful

John F. Wade
Arr. by Margaret Goldston

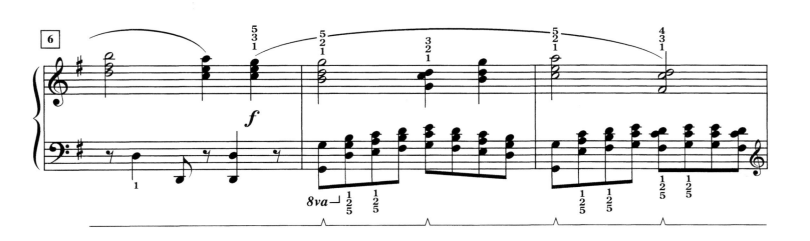

24

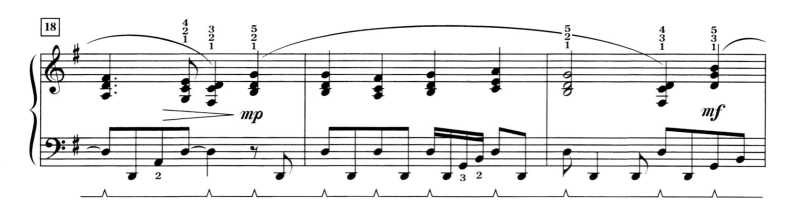

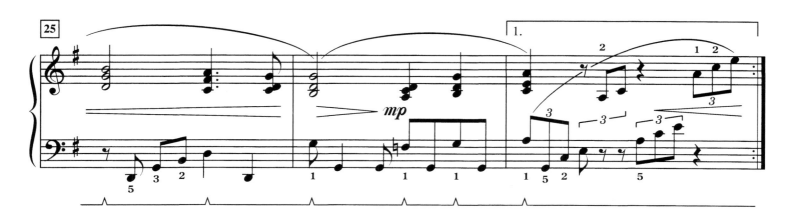

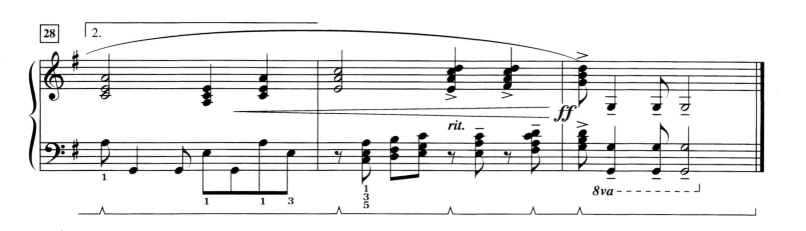

O Holy Night

Adolphe C. Adam
Arr. by Margaret Goldston

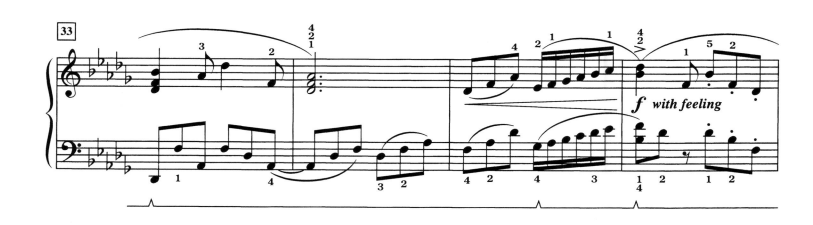

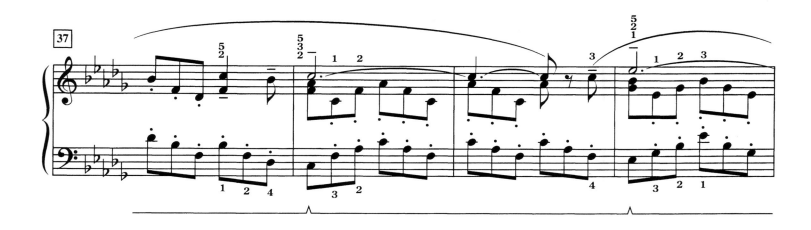

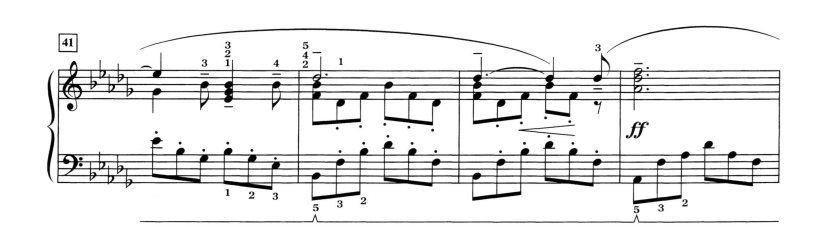

Go, Tell It on the Mountain

African-American Spiritual
Arr. by Margaret Goldston

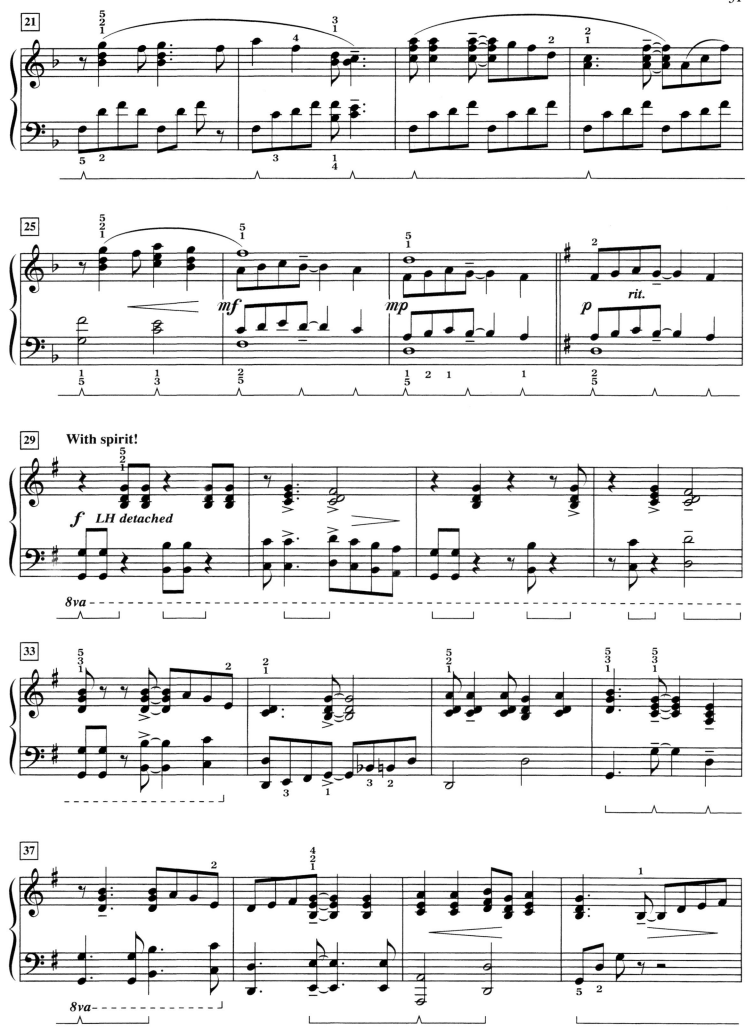